the
tender *Wild*
things

the tender Wild things

by Diane Jarvenpa

Many
Voices
Project
Winner

© 2007 by Diane Jarvenpa
First Edition
Library of Congress Control Number: 2006928670
ISBN-10: 0-89823-236-8
ISBN-13: 978-0-89823-236-3
MVP Number 113
Cover design and interior book design by Sarah Teveldal
Author photograph by Nick Lethert

The publication of *The Tender Wild Things* is made possible by the generous support of the Jerome Foundation and other contributors to New Rivers Press.

For academic permission please contact Frederick T. Courtright at 570-839-7477 or permdude@eclipse.net. For all other permissions, contact The Copyright Clearance Center at 978-750-8400 or info@copyright.com.

New Rivers Press is a nonprofit literary press associated with
Minnesota State University Moorhead.

Wayne Gudmundson, Director
Alan Davis, Senior Editor
Thom Tammaro, Poetry Editor
Liz Severn, Fiction Editor
Donna Carlson, Managing Editor
     Managerial Assistants: Jennifer Bakken, Cassie Tweten
     The Tender Wild Things book team: Jay Bordt, Ellie Musselman, Jay Patrick,
          Abby Peterson
     Editorial Interns: Jay Bordt, Jennifer Costley, Suzzanne Kelley, Erik Meyer,
          Ellie Musselman, Jay Patrick, Abby Peterson, Laura Qualey
     Design Interns: Nicole Anacker, Lexis Graap, Brian Koch, Sarah Teveldal
     Festival Coordinator: Heather Steinmann
Allen Sheets, Design Manager
Deb Hval, Business Manager

Printed in the United States of America.

New Rivers Press
c/o MSUM
1104 7th Avenue South
Moorhead, MN 56563
www. newriverspress.com

Lilialle, minun hennolle villikukkaselleni

Contents

Hunger

Twelve Moons

Driving Across Finland

The Long Deliberation of the Body

Star Moving Through Nine Heavens

Go to the forest
Go to the mountains
Go to the far off sea
Let loneliness
caress you
until your skin is thin enough
So thin that your heart
sees me through it
that I was the one
who caressed you,
who caresses you
Go, go.

–Tommy Tabermann
trans. Börje Vähämäki

Hunger

Hunger

Each time the hungry crows light on the freeway fence
I think of how we make a stab at feeding ourselves,
how we reinvent our gardens when we can;
lima beans and cantaloupe in R. L. Stevenson's Samoa,
shallow running Japanese vegetables in Belgium,
Hmong-grown banana peppers and lemongrass in Minnesota.
But it goes deeper than the gut, this hunger,
this yearning and sorrow that balloons to fill all spaces
making us reel and wobble in the wake of its imbalance,
it is why we flap our arms, if only in our dreams,
to try for flight, talk to God, voyage into wilderness.
It is why the Russian Guitar Poets passed their songs
through the factory underground,
why Strauss, paralyzed with fear, still rode trains across America,
or why my great-aunt Cecilia pressed birth control
into the hands of tired mothers and performed in Finnish plays
for immigrants in 1920s iron ore mining towns.
It is the drunken song of all of us, longing beneath the stars.
Shucking crayfish in Louisiana, digging sugar beets in North Dakota,
starching uniforms for the hotel kitchen workers,
our days stream by a baptism of work;
minds numb, bellies satiated but still empty.
At night an incarnation of rituals sweeps across countertops,
cooking fires and oil-polished hard wood tables.
Here we share, pray, and taste small bits of heaven.
When we can take time,
let it spill slowly from our fingers
like so many peas into a wooden bowl,
we find moonlight in the copper pot,
snowdrops in the milk bottle,
we find sadness and we find glory too.
When we sit down and dine
on hard bread and onions,

rutabaga or blue corn cakes,

we wrap up our stones of worry

and set them out back by the stacks of old firewood.

Each day we are hungry, you and I,

tongues dry, lips white,

we reach for each other and we taste it all,

bitter and sweet, it floods our mouths.

The Tango Dancers

Scent of rose musk and green lavender
rises as the dancers pass by,
their embrace closer than braided ribbons,
a vow to let the space between them
drop away with the ash from a cigarette they step out.
Pressed hip bone to hip bone, rib to rib,
they turn and spin, legs kissing legs,
pulling the elixir of the dotted eighth notes
up from their feet like tap roots.
And there is that other scent,
a violent scent, the spike of her heel
spearing secrets between his legs.
Each body is the memory shadow of the other
moving across the floor. The only speech
in the wrists, hips, and ankles,
the back a cello string they finger and bend.
"The Violet Seller" plays its accordion
of single reed stops into their bones,
a scattering of light and heat unhurried.
This is about holding a woman, holding a man,
about the simple distance between us,
how difficult and how easy it is to fill.

George Sand and Frederic Chopin in Majorca

Valldemosa, Spain

Her daily walks take her past
the cypress and the Barbary figs,

the ruby dates tucked high into palms,
olive trees fingering deep pink sky,

the tinkling of shepherd bells
from the distant grapefruit hills.

While inside, Latin prayers instruct the walls,
incense and balsam fight the smoking stove

and the large Gothic throne casts
pointy shadows on the wall in lantern light.

She knows he rests in the cold,
wrapped in wadded calico,

lungs heavy,
moths falling from candle flame

as he spells preludes across the mind's keyboard,
hands flying and resting like pale birds.

And all along his indifferent sky,
the astonishing music of denial.

Following the Stevensons

Calistoga, California

There are days in a life when thus to climb out of the lowlands,
seems like scaling heaven.
                    —R. L. Stevenson

Hiking the switchback trails,
sweet bay trees and redwoods tangle and stud
the cliffy shoulders of Mount St. Helena,
the fragrant chaparral holds pale moths
that spread and close their wings
like children's hands making prayers.
Silence mists upon the hills,
the taste of pine resin on their tongues.
and the dust off the madrone in their hair
as Louis boils the morning coffee
and Fanny steps around the triple tier of beds.
Red rock brawls down a ravine as though tossed
in disappointment and forgotten.

A path of nutmeg, cinnebar, azalea and calcanthus
brought the honeymooners here
to sleep on hay beds, breathe the piney wood,
cut their boots on sharp red stones,
sunbathe among the nests of rattlers.
Sunshine sparkles like quartz,
hour melts insensibly into hour,
their other lives fixed and frozen
back in their lowland homes.
The rich passivity of nature
measures them for neglect and survival,
voyages taken so they can see
that different spark buried deep inside,
the spark that keeps them together
closer than two pennies in a pocket.

Sea fogs roll in,
winds grumble in the canyon,
move the jeweled treetops in silence,
the way a song can't be heard
but remains singing in the ear.
The blacksmith's forge filled with dead leaves
burns bright as they climb to bunks under open sky.

Over the years
they discover perching jay and burr patch,
barbadine, mummy apple and kava root,
every new syllable, counter-motion and bird-like
continent of the other, beginning in Monterey
and ending in Samoa.
Ever mindful of mortality,
they pull together
a ship of their own making,
tasting the new alphabet
written across their sails.
It tastes of past, of future,
of something finer.

Charmain London Wishes Her Husband Jack a Happy Birthday

Because when I see you,
I sing silently to the little boy
with a few pocketed coins
and inked stamps.
What music loud enough or sweet
to spend or lick their dreams?

Because when I read you,
it is a prelude to back-alley rhymes,
simple bolts of speech unrolled and set
unhesitating into river valleys
or piled like silver snow into a coal car
and spilled onto the black night,
just the hard corners of stars for competition.

Because when I touch you,
it is my skeptical heart
that suddenly believes
parakeets flocked the Kansas osage,
that Antarctica once held Australia,
that gymnosperms have seen it all.

Because when I smell you,
it is cotton and linen,
corn tassels and black pansy,
soft leather and green apples.

Because when I taste you,
I taste pilgrimage and invention,
mineral salts and peaches,
lifelines wrinkling and smoothing,
dust and honey.

Because the good years have gathered
like common lilies,
like spring thaw in a narrow river,
like a whistling of birds
you don't have to count.

Because I know
I can't stop you,
because this is
your cup of tea,
your pitcher of beer,
your ocean park—
drink it up.
Here, let me help.

Cheers.

Elvira Puccini's Different Dream

Sometimes I arrive here
a boat that bumps a seawall,
and I get out,
my legs two sail kites
that carry me across your land,
the one I can't really know,
the one that has its own dreams
of young maidens in lakes,
young maidens with voices of songbirds.
Where time is a weightless wisdom
that you keep in your pocket,
not a watch,
but a kind of seed or kiss
that opens the unknown.
And there I am
hovering over your dream,
the one where maybe I appear,
but probably it is someone else,
another woman
rising from that lake,
water streaming down her legs.
And all I can do is turn away,
return to my boat,
to my own dream
where water is first born,
where it is sometimes clear and deep.

Someone Loved This Painting Once

The artist Murillo in Seville
mixing dark bowls of prayer,
paint blind and blurry in their pots,
thick impasto from the palette
made into moon and lamb,
grass blades and rushing seas,
the infant shepherd with too-soft eyes
telling us he knows the face of God.

The Austrian painter in her smock
stretching canvas, blending color,
standing on the marble floor
copying breath for breath each brushstroke,
the moon, the thicketwood,
the boy and his lamb.

The older man
pointing to the painting in the museum
asking for one of his own
that he may remember
where he was when he first met her,
a bloom of laurel in her painter's gown.
Together they eat the fruit
of a dozen still lifes each night
upon the brick-warmed sheets.

The daughter of the man
hanging the painting over her fireplace,
its fire's long flames no match for
the scumbling of painted light
as if sun dogs and spun silk

rise from the body of the lamb.
She finds comfort during the war
in the delicate cherub-boy face,
finds sanctuary in the far-off blue mountains.

The couple who have lived together
over twenty years
adding to the hunted clutter of their lives
the paint globs made mud and flesh,
the cool blue-wooded dusk
holding the pink boy and the golden lamb,
two strange sparks in a dreary world,
their small bells of praise sent deep into the trees.
A song the couple sometimes hears
as they reach into their nights,
the soft maps detailed inside their palms
unfolded and released,
the thoughtful, careful turns
of pigment, light, and shape
slowly coming into view.

René and Odette

Notre Dame de Laval, France

Up inside the hill's sweet center
they suffer the spiny urchins
to pluck glossy bulbs of chestnuts,

point to balloons of mistletoe, accepting
their invasive emblems of love, cup hands
beneath the spring that cuts between the heather,

wade knee deep in the curved blade of the river
as it shines a sharp edge through old farms
where they stand still for the birds.

Safe from downpours that slicken slate,
their discreet audience of cats
is offered as constant frescoes of shadow

and from snaggles of thorns and mud,
bilberries, mushrooms and quince appear
in bowls alongside clutter of another time—

rocks worn to fingerlings
bearing tinctures of ocean,
tin toys and chocolate molds.

They are getting old, they say,
but still they shimmer like cicadas
in the woodskin pockets of each room

that houses five centuries
of hands sweeping cobwebs,
looking onto green fields where

the long deliberation of the body
and new-mown hay
deliver answers,

where they lay down on a map
of spent wings and let the fresh light
fill their slender bones.

Twelve Moons

A Map of My World

Sketching my way through the parts of each day,
I thread a line of passage to work,
my Volkswagon calculating distance across the river
and down into the valley of sheep and herons.

I debranch the line of trajectory
to my desktop, voices quelling at the doorway
and at the meeting table and later where everyone
impatiently queues up for bags of hot food.

The car engine's exhaust powders a vein home,
south of the Lakota settlements, near the orphanage
and the ghost streets cut out like old tree stumps,
replaced with the full trench of the interstate.

I measure distance from garden to spigot,
mark the place the doves mate in the roof gutter,
note where cat feet have printed countertops above
the old mouse trap, still holding a tiny spoon of cheese.

This small planet on which I spin
has no gilded calligraphy,
it's just the ancient plain of a tired woman
whose faith and failing twin themselves
daily in the office and in that slim Lutheran heaven,
a refuge at times too narrow for all of its economies.

Alone and off-center
to the latitude and longitude of another day
I watch the rivers flood to the treetops
and the comet shoot three-tail plumage
across my backyard sky,
making its own new map

and the doves up there too,
in the quartermoon dark,
perched into the winds, my envy
in their gathering and release
that is all their power
and I'm down below,
my eye a steady bead
on all these silent movements,
trying to keep a fix
on their arc and blur.

Alignment

Five planets line up
across the night sky,
a convergence of orbits in a row.
On this planet we like our lines,
always and forever assembling them,
the tips of hyacinths at the garden wall,
acres of corn, alfalfa, soybeans,
spools in the Carolina cotton mill,
meeting of the rails at Promontory Point.
All those rows of gunworks,
series of canon balls, soldiers in advance, retreat,
different from the line of that ant colony
threading its way along the finer coasts of Italy.
The line of cattle that followed my path
following the country dog down to the icy river
and the windmills madly blading the blue sky
lined up to collect the wind that cut sharp
across that pipestone plain.
And all the lines on all those maps
that point us where we'd like to go,
Amor de Dios, Crane Mountain, Nightingale Island.
There was that line that joined my husband's parents
before the justice of the peace,
dressed in Sunday best, witnesses flanking this newly
declared union, a tender column of hope in the chaos
and defeat of the Great Depression
and the trajectory of his father's sperm traveling
its hot course to his mother's waiting egg
during the last year of WWII to result
in their third son who loved the blue lines
on the ruled school paper,
where he would later
stand at his own blackboard

drawing long marks which were maps
where he fit the suddenly vivid
towns and rivers of Tanzania and Brazil.
As the planets rise in the sky,
distant nails in a barn roof rafter,
we take a look at this display long in the making.
This line required no tools from the shed,
no compass or cartographer's pen,
just decades of travel and steady purpose,
the weighty message balanced high:
No matter what—proceed,
their spin echoing over us like bells.

The Accident of Clouds

I remember laying my bony nine-year-old
self in the thick grass, green as emerald silk
that grew in the shade
on the north side of our house, clouds
passing over, wondering where they
were going, who they were passing over next.

Dylan was out there somewhere
singing "John Wesley Harding,"
presidential campaigners were doing their best to ignore
the rising chants of protesting students,
my future husband hitchhiking Europe
was possibly measuring the full personal impact
of British driving on the left,
his head quickly finding the pavement.

I remember putting on my new granny glasses,
the clouds now bursts of lilacs against the sky's
great swimming pool of violet, wondering
what it would be like to see a real violet sky,
not the kind on science fiction television
where men in odd-fitting space suits
walked on poorly carved styrofoam planets,
but the kind my pen pal described
when she was on holiday at the sea.
She was a woman. Men fought over her.
She was eleven. She was French.

And the man I would marry
suffered Scottish breakfasts,
followed Swedish fishing boats,
circled cathedrals in the rain,
unfolded worn maps on top of stone bridges

deciding whether to take a right or a left
at the public garden, the porcelain museum,
every pub that sold Scotch eggs and warm beer.
He walked alone for miles on cool September days,
his young body knowledgeable in all its fine new pain.

If he looked up at the clouds and wondered
where they were going, his thoughts would
have probably taken them across the North Sea,
pressed by winds over Jutland to form sleet
and thin down again to nothing over the Caspian,
never to a little girl guessing at life,
watching clouds pass and build,
noticing how some met to form new ones
shaped like writing tablets, sugar bowls,
sailboats heading for the sun,
wondering how long their journey had been,
the different lives they'd led
before a random westerly gathered and pushed them
into an unknown stretch of blue.

Around this House

a tiny piece of land
weedy with mud,
strewn with iris,
rock piles,
woodpeckers knocking
in the dead elm tree.

The brown paper bag
under the wooden step
holds the perfect white network
of sparrow bones.
We're not much for burials,
absence is a squatter
across too many of our days.

Wind blows hair,
dirt cakes hands and feet,
cut grass sits in small mounds
to kick around the bald spots.
The immense pines groan,
old men in a softball game
raising their gloves
awkwardly palming
the stray warbler.

Sun rises and falls
around this house,
around its loam and rock,
bonemeal and sheep shit,
around the wordless
twisted fingers
of the linden trees
as they drop spring seeds
onto the broken sidewalk

where the clover
and summer pigweed blooms,
where your hands reach
for the linden flowers,
where your hands pour
the rich red mulberries into mine
mixing together with the scent
of our own small histories
as we let them drop and fade away.

The Collectors

Cinnabar, lava, blue slate, agate,
old sea bottom mud,
door stops and lake skippers.

Urchin spike, oyster,
sea button, pin-dot winkle,
salt coins jangling in pockets.

Bones and veins of winter hills,
sage, bittersweet, foxtail, hawkweed,
chill-bleached, dusty crisp in pressed glass.

Soup bowls, china cups and pitchers
filled with lemon water, thick cream,
brewed leaf sipped from worn spoons.

Wood-chewed skins, seedling ink marks,
wing and belly vowels, black serpent trails,
stories stacked, falling like prophet stars.

This is the place we attach all tangents and spoils,
the old house sinking into its flood plane,
our globe drawn imperfect pole down to pole

with someone's tossed garden bamboo,
the antique ring equator good gold for a tooth,
the Mexican hammock a woven isthmus between trees.

Boxes and bowls, drawers and jars,
packed tight, can't overlook, don't throw out,
in darkest recesses spell—never give up.

For in one most perfect dream
singing birds come and go from the gap-toothed cages
and our neighbors skillfully play all the busted ukuleles

as we and the children run to the river
in our flower-printed shirts
and let all the tiny ships slip free from their bottles.

Digging Lupines

The long rippling hill of blue
rises from the ditch down the road
from the old outhouse.
I am bent at the side of the highway,
mud pooling to my knees
as I take the world's most blunt trowel
and furrow in trying to reach the black cloud,
subterranean network of blind fingers
clasping the sweet meat of worms
and soil full of Lake Superior rain.

Each summer the lupine break out from ditch stubble,
waving their blown hollowed bits of shell
and this year I am ready with my ice cream bucket,
it is cold and I want to harvest them
into the bed of my own garden, such as it is,
where the cats pee, the weeds ripen
and the crows look for dead mice,
where the blues is a song the grass would sing—
if I had any grass, that is.

And so it is only right to dig a hole
and dig another and pour them in,
blue and ordinary as hard rain
washing and giving drink
to the one from the city
who comes to walk
in highway grass,
who comes to steal
the tender wild things.

The Visit

It is a constant mumble of prayers
as they drop the finer snow of pollen,
head-rub the lily cup,
pull syrup from each precinct of thistle,

shutter themselves in pear, plum, and cherry
before the old stars are shed on the hillside,
where wooly vapors of the sea
snag in new leaves, in her hair,

in the spun glass of his wings
as they fall from sky,
tied together in a knot,
rolling their ball

of stingers and golden milk
around the bed of foxglove, to rise
and fall into my lap,
the tight circle of their bodies

clamped and insistent,
union of sun and egg
I hold buzzing in my palm
until they spread four wings

and rise, tiny planet,
fist of love and death,
their hum a furious ambition I listen to
as long as I can until it fades out past the hay bales.

The Way Birds Build the World

For Alan Jarvenpa

From our data we suspect the songbird
dreams of singing.
   —Daniel Margoliash

We hear their migrant language
as two halves of star and rock
for that is all we can make of it,
we who sit on slopes,
bushwhacked and sober,
mystified by their flyways,
making us minions to the tree tops,
those nurseries strung like so many cups
and saucers filled with the new moon,
its scimitar crafting new wings.

Who doesn't want to know
that sleep found deep inside leaves?
In our youth we braved scars
searching nests for newborns
tucked inside woven moss,
snakeskins on which to lay our own heads,
to dream how morning can swarm over
with whirlings of hawks, geese skeins,
marbled godwits, golden plovers.

And all that singing
that we know is less proverb
than work manual,
but still to us is oratory.
Here is an apple!
Taste this plum!

What is greater than the worm,
the wild fig, the cherry,
this stand of hawthorn,
this crest, this ruff, this tail?

In our dreams
we always fly,
circling our houses,
skimming the chain-link, ball fields
dropping away like canyons.
In our dreams
we are the shearwaters
clerking ocean maps,

the arctic terns
always seeing the sun.
In our dreams
we are the doves,
the true believers
leaving eggs on fire escapes
despite all the noise
and fire and dark.

Tuula's Nettle Soup

The long tail of early summer
sweeps its clean, dry threads
around the porch, around the table

and at each place with its white bowl
filled with nettle soup.
Each bowl unfurls a sweet spell

like the head of a fern, each bowl
filled with bits of cloud,
sea foam and forest.

As we eat, the language of grass
and the flat arctic woods
become clearer in the moonlight,

syllables grow in our mouths,
familiar movements
of reed and water

on the earth's floor
spin in the spoon
that softness there.

As we learn to speak our lines,
the earth gives up
a little more of itself.

Night Walk to the Sauna

This is all chicory and cold shale,
wormwood and shinleaf
where my mother holds high the lantern

to step around the wasp nest
and stinging nettles.
Through the humid night

dense and prickly as thimbleberries,
along this path where owls scissor mice
and the bats staccato-dive insect clouds.

We move slowly for the old pines
send out tentacle roots
and the low catch of spider webs

stitch sudden death blooms.
We follow the lake scent of iron and fish scale
to the sweet dry smoke of birch

where my mother feeds the fire her old sorrows
in the small, wooden room,
where I come out of the long darkness,

eyes filmy, hair sea of green, feet of thorns
and shed my little girl meanness,
that tight slick slide of shell

to a wash of gold and pink,
lungs of steam,
awkward limbs filled with new, slim muscle.

And my mother all hawkweed clean,
our two pumping hearts like one
blood moon rising higher,

our thirsty bones hissing stars
through the wild mint
and that acre of lake that lets us drink.

Twelve Moons

yī

I sweep the Northern Dipper off the front step,
galaxies of ice gather in your hair.

èr

A cardinal appears in the empty lilac,
for a valentine we thaw a summer cherry pie.

sān

Gathering pinecones to set by our bed,
a future of trees fragrant in our dreams.

sì

Many bowls catch hours of sweet rain,
you simmer spring clouds with watercress and lemon.

wǔ

Ils sont chantent une rivière. Hirondelle des Fenêtre,
Tarin des Aulnes, Héron Cendré, Martin Pêcheur.

liù

Drinking wine beneath the June plum tree,
hedgehogs grumble at us in the midnight grass.

qī

Praying to the thistle and the sunflower,
goldfinches tell silent stories at the feeder.

bā

Our silver-blue remembering and forgetting
and the dragonfly's wings, cool the hot, green day.

jiŭ

Whitefish leap at drifts of tiny flies,
your kite floats from your pocket, a distant god.

shí

Moon rises over empty hearts,
in our grief we cannot find its delicate color.

shíyī

I bake apples, pears and figs,
honey for the tongue in the dark November belly.

shíèr

You pass me small candles to plant in the trees,
a settling of wings lights each bough.

Driving Across
Finland

In The Deep Woods

This is where my grandmother
came to pick mushrooms
in her new country,

belly empty, mind scattered,
mud and tears slick on her boots.
Here in the deep woods

she came to loosen pain,
break it off of its wheel,
let it drop off her skin

with the old rotting trunks of aspen.
She walked under thunderheads,
around bramble fires and the thumbprints

of early floods, the whirlpooling eddies
and foam soaking her skirts.
After the drowning white of winter,

she came to find carpets of twinflowers
spreading across snow-soaked hills.
Here she tasted liquor on her lips

of wintergreen and red raspberry,
sap of sugar maples,
the sweet and the bitter

flowing inside her,
filling the vacuum of regret.
This is where she came

stepping quietly into the deep woods,
thorns gripping, mayflies billowing,
sitting alone on that old stump

at the center of the New World,
spellbound by its strange,
imperfect land.

Watching the small birds
in their delicate nests, understanding
their sudden, brilliant flash of wing.

Sketchbook of the Trapper's Wife

When I'm alone and have time on my hands
I flatten birch skins between warm stones
and sketch with alder, bloodroot, and wild plum.

This is the pine out front standing roots in sand,
marsh grass softened by mouths of birds,
the river struck gold by sun death.

Here, this is where we skied the log trails
in the lung-piercing scatter of snow
and this is when the summer windstorm
flung trees into broken bones.

Farther on, there is wild rice from the wet month
we had to walk the beaver dam and a feather from
the time the eagle sat sick for days in the dead aspen.

On these pages I stopped drawing altogether.
Winter sat heavy, long black nights, banked with clouds.
I cut disks from cottonwood twigs, glued them
with pine pitch. Stars for the long empty nights.

Here we spilled the chokecherry wine,
trout jumped all day, the full bladders of toads
sang of midsummer, a stray cow wandered over
from a far-off field. I slept in a hedge of bindweed.

These pages are the dead.
Raccoon, rabbit, muskrat, gray fox, deer,
turtle, pheasant, beaver, bear.

And these pages are the future;
no jackknives, no pelts hanging in the sun,

no ungainly speech or artless mourning,
only mounds of snow, clean and waiting

for the steelheads, for the slippery elm,
for the greening of nettles,
for all that stinks and chafes and blinds,
for all that breaks open in the chest and sings.

Warming the Center

Great-aunt Lydia liked to watch
the black wings of birds
bear down over the back lots of her small town
as she wished for a brief rewind to summer,
a last chance at begging fruit from the garden.

But there they were, the red currants
like hard beads from a kid's necklace
and the pickling cucumbers
soft from the ice-bone frost.

She didn't seem to mind the leafless trees,
dark arthritic fingers pointing at the moon,
the cornfield stubble without its perfect food
or the sky now expanded to fill up her picture window,
filling her widow lungs with the shivering of stars.

Still it seemed only right to try to keep it all at bay,
unfolding the tattered linen sheets,
the same kind her mother used to clean with lemon
and set out across the rye fields,
only now they covered the rose bushes at night,
thin cloths of hope, laid on gently the same way
she set dough across the tops of her rutabaga pies,

the same way her small hands
rested on top of her cold mother
lost after a hard fall on the frozen lake—
as if coaxing some bloom.

Driving Across Finland

Past baby moose,
their slim young legs all bone and hinges,
I hum through place names that
are shaken from a cup of Scrabble tiles;
Vuolijoki, Kokkola, Ylikiiminki.
I follow hawks and magpies
across the birch-skin-paper scroll of sky,
hayfields rolling away, breakers on an ocean
and the poppy-red barns fishing boats in the mist.
Reindeer gathering by swamps of green

scatter time and place with the lichen and stones.
Tupasvilla lather out of the ground
like milkweed among the nettles.
I share nothing with the white night
except potato fields and the watery wood
holding a thin pine-needle moon.
And I look deep into the trees,

the way they dissolve trunk into trunk
through the open window.
How I study their assemblage
searching for signs, for clues
like the young maiden searching
in the storybook woods for the door
that leads to her captured loved ones.
Only my loved ones weren't captured,

they left this place, filled carpet bags
with village linen, empty pockets
for a future world. And that was it.
They were gone.
All these trees merely thorns

pricking their dreams,
and these winds the odd forgotten
melody of their mother's songs.

And how even after seven decades
of being away
I saw something in their eyes
which I see now.
It isn't only the indigo sea,
weary yet alive, but also
the morning gray-smoke sky
filled with migrating birds swelling
the air with sorrow, their din
in the hearts of everything.

Fish Father

Kneeling beside a puzzle of heron bones
and deposits of wolf scat
you took turns with the stars playing midwife,
releasing the small fingerlings into the river.

The coterie of shadow skimmers
made vacant rivers whole,
slivers of sky
filled with fish-scale moons.

You said how in your dreams
you were lifted by gusts
and set down at the river
with your brothers,

the one who outlived you,
the one who disappeared,
drifted off into the Great Dust Bowl
leaving behind only a single jar of wooden lures.

How you all kneeled at the river
with homemade birch poles
watching the sun spread golden wings
across tamarack and fireweed,

the fish slowly moving toward that light,
those same fish that called to you
rubbing their fins on stones,
angels of transmutation.

The simple curve of brown and rainbow
passed each other often out there
where you seeded them, your body separate
from the undercurrent of that silver breathing

until you held one beating in your hands
and knew once again the silent, wild cry
of a different sort of living, standing
alone at the river's edge.

Osteichthyes

After the hydrofoil skimmed the surface of Lake Baikal
they set me down to a plate of blini and arctic grayling,
the smoked fish fat sweet on my fingertips
and I found myself thinking about all the carp,
northerns, muskies and lake trout I've been a party to,
all those silver darters collected in a bucket, on a boat floor,
inside a gill net, from camp stove to tasty meat on tongues.
My childhood was rich with supple worms and minnows
so I could snag my first, second, and third bullhead
and witness how long they lived outside their waters
gasping what seemed like forever
until one of us kids hit them on the head with a shoe.
We didn't care how long the young were protected
by the males, we knew they liked muddy lakes and so did we.
All those days catching sunnies with my dad
was conversation without words, what do you say to a little girl
who refuses to go to church? Make her remove barbs
from the pierced flesh, say a quick prayer before eating.
On my honeymoon in Juneau I caught a Dolly Varden,
wasn't this what love was? Shivering in a boat,
eating Kentucky Fried Chicken, that sincere waiting for a line tug?
And that is the secret, isn't it, about fishing and sex,
the proper response and the timing?
Isn't it always about timing?
One day my brother took me out to the middle of my street
to show me how to use a fly rod, the golden whip
of *e*'s and *u*'s over tar and gravel
only to have a poet take me out to a trout stream
just so my baffled hands could set my catch free,
pat it on its speckled sides and let it flex on
through reeds and not on hooks.
If you are ever out Irkutsk way
I do recommend the limnological museum,

many handsome fish on display, long since extinct.
Ones with what look like legs
and others with gills like blossoms
that swam in the mile-deep motions of that lake.
Perhaps had someone released them into the dark blue waves
instead of hitting them on the head with Russian shoes
they'd still be gliding around down there.
And instead of dipping my fingers into smoky fat
I'd be simply dipping my hands into cold arctic water,
taking on gills and fins like a salmon maiden,
swimming for my life.

Aquarium

I have felt this before,
this motion without moving,
following sunshot clouds
ticking away over my head.
It could be a wild orchard
and this, the fence line, keeping me apart
from the confusion of fruit and flower
in some place like Madagascar.

A different world,
where slivers of lemon,
pocket bibles and pen knives
nibble at gravel,
fly through kelp skirts
and the curly horns of coral.
It is a flight of trumpets,
parrots and butterflies,
damsels and bandits,
idols and goats.

And I study their habitual,
unblinking instinct
to chart sea maps inside a tank,
converting my sorrows,
small and pitiful as they are, into
some kind of acceptance for the moment.
The confined, fluorescent water,
an ancient shifting of tides
that gathers the fragile and the radiant
into a sudden pattern of connection.
Like that day in the nursing home
when my mother loudly sang
the *Internationale*,

the whole table of demented women
smiling and humming along.

Here at the aquarium
I want to breathe
the strange water bubbling
back, a kind of birth,
an erasure, a dim memory.
Could be a garden, could be
clouds, could be rain.

With Mother in the Library

The light was different there,
the muddy gray
of shells on a foggy beach,
discoveries you stumble across and stop
to study, rolling the grits in your hand.
She rocked the books in her palms,
the breath of pages passing through
the body at the wrists.
She passed them onto me,
sentences swirling in the air with ink fibers
released from their bindings,
hanging like Spanish moss
at doorways, along window sills,
entangling in the nightly janitor's broom.
A giant humidor of words and pictures
picked over, rolled on carts
and placed onto shelves with care,
just so she and I could choose one
and turn a page,
striking a slow-moving storm
dragging its tail over the frozen sea
of our quiet lives
into fire.

Dreaming of Father

It is his light moon
presence that I first notice
in my dreams.

This is what wakes me up,
his quiet monk's voice
uttering my name like a fog drift.

Biologist and second-grade girl
joined at the silent kitchen table
with our tea and hot chocolate.

And soon after
having been bundled
into the extra weavings of wool,

the shiny spring bindings
taut across my red rubber boots,
he stands me at the top of the hill.

This is where the sleep
finally leaves my small bones
and I stand alone in a cold puff of smoke

as he cuts his skis into new country snow,
his broad back growing little-boy small,
insisting a map for me to follow.

And I follow him down in simple terror,
the wasps and wild mint frozen over
where he stands willing my faith.

Sometimes I fly,
my body crossing clouds,
skylarks for ankles.

Mostly I crash,
a beetle caught on its back,
the shimmering flecks

of the crosshatched hill on my tongue
as he liberates limbs and rescues lost mittens,
the December light pearling my lashes

and the wind raising white stars off the fir boughs
all along that morning hill where he lifts me up
offering me again the only god he knows.

Finlandia

My mother listened to *Finlandia*
like some men have a double scotch neat,
an exit door from hours spent in a fluorescent-lit room.
It was a defiance,
unwinding to a thick bravado of horns.
After hours of being someone's secretary
she would gently remove that black moon
of Sibelius from its cardboard sleeve,
close her eyes and she was gone.
My mother tapped a typewriter with an unnatural speed
as though she was behind the wheel of a race car
slamming into the occasional barrier wall.
This was not music. There was no message
from Beethoven on his sickbed thanking god,
hidden between the carbons.
My mother chanted *Kalevala*
in a language that tricked birds from nests,
bewildered stars to new positions.
Her voice could be heard singing
in the backyard while beating the carpets,
all songs of her youth about gypsies, vagabonds,
and endless summer nights.
While my father studied viable streambeds;
my one brother smoked weed, the other
diagrammed matrilineal kinships,
and I spied on my mother
as she sat head bent over her coffee cup,
lost in a music that was loud and gusty,
but also had a low, mournful pulling away
that made me think of empty row boats rocking over waves.
And she would look up and see me and I would go to her
and together we sat in her lonely boat.
I suppose she wanted me to see the red berries

her mother was picking on the summer hillside,
her father walking with his sisters
across the winter lake, but all I saw was my mother
the chill of gray stealing through her hair,
her sad face, calm and full,
the music slowly moving through her body
filling her with secrets.

The Old Sea

We never really saw them do this, our parents,
but I suppose we look much like them,
sand in aging toes, wind lifting gray hairs
off damp necks as we walk the shore
letting old arguments fall away with our footprints.

The last time I saw your parents together in the old house
they were scooping up gigantic bowls of ice cream
with cherries on a warm September night,
and even though they both were dying,
they cracked jokes at the other's expense,
saving the chewed pits, the prolonged annoyance
of each other keeping them going.

The last time I saw my parents together in their apartment
they were making chicken soup. My father tore the meat
and while we waited for the broth to simmer
my mother gave him chocolate so he wouldn't have to sneak it,
his dementia wild with sweet hungers.
A decade earlier their marriage all but disappearing,
just ghost dragging ghost from blame turned mythic.

For fifty years our parents rinsed each others' pale skin
in sun warmth, in hospital bed,
marriage at times the slow damp fog of night,
a gathering and a relinquishing.
It rolled in blue, thinned out silver,
tasted of many moons, storms,
hidden deaths, cast-out pearls,
a fresh-water shock of disappointments
and a secret balance of worlds
like this inlet,
a shining, wounded place

shaking loose small ruins of the planet,
sea-whipped and salt-rubbed,
those glistened bits and bones of hope
scattered at our feet.

*The Long
Deliberation
of the Body*

Mother Writing

Some days it seemed as if she was
the lisianthus, small white bud ready to let go
the blue-flower speech into the warm night,
her spreading petals lush
against the skin of summer,
the pure act of bloom.

Other days she was a man-of-war,
all business, main mast, keel and gunport,
spearing her navigation.
All night watch and log line,
no idlers of the idle kind,
just battle stations with plenty of breastwork,
hole plugging and the occasional
chain shot if necessary.

And even in the wreckage of her warship,
exhausted and barely afloat,
no matter how many
countless nights she had seen it,
her astonishment at the way the Milky Way
raises its creamy ribbon light from the black
as if coming into view for the very first time.

Ikebana

In my mother's hands the fragrance still
of pine cone, black walnut, honeycomb,
the lampwicks of green willow.

She has placed a toadstool,
rotted old stump under birch leaves,
above the sky stretches the moon's collarbone.

Chokecherry and bittersweet
are pulled and shaped into sleek winds,
a sunflower opens its aboriginal star.

Half wet and scented by the Big Dipper,
granite mountain and sweet pea vines
vibrate with the fresh light.

A cloud in a pond,
an egret drifts in on a wisp of frost,
tastes the fallen tears.

Mother Tongue

At first it was your secret,
a spice box you closed up tight.

Eventually exotic unknown strands
spilled out and you gave it all away

as your face measured each sentence,
strained over the hum of bitter verbs,

relaxed as family names and towns
came to the tongue hard won.

Now parts of your speech shuffle wildly,
words exiled to live inside

your body a different life.
Unread books pile up on your bed,

photos tucked into every corner of your room
gleam for the immortal bodies in them.

There is an old blue dress you finger
as you chant the language of your parents:

taas muistot nuo syttyvät palamaan
elon tummaa taivasta valaisemaan.

The hour before has blown
away like cottonwood seed,

but the back counter of your father's
butcher shop with its reddened paper

comes into full view.
You tell me the story again

and tell it once more and I
don't know what else to do

but take your words to my own mouth as food
as if this eating could stop your hunger.

Translation of the Finnish:

memories light and flame,
brighten the dark skies of life.

A Wish for Fruit

The Alzheimer's nurse bats an orange balloon
around the room. Clara, Winnie, Frances, Juvey,
and Flora all take turns hitting it back.
When it's her turn the balloon lands on her lap
and drops off. She stares at it in disappointment,
not because she didn't hit it, in fact she brushed it off
as though it were some unwanted lint or crumbs.
She looks at me as though she is making some
endless fall through space where every known part
of her is rapidly being forgotten and all that is left
is her wheelchair and the dull rubber
vessel filled with air, bobbing at her feet.
The therapist asks her to kick it and she kicks it hard
and I know it is the woman with the white lab coat
she wants to kick. She waves me over and whispers
something that sounds like cloudberry.
And I think, why not ripe cloudberries?
Their golden thimbles set into her hands,
the tart drops melting on her tongue,
a small bit of golden juice she can swallow
that answers the unforgotten longing for other worlds.

Stealing Seeds

Sometimes when I wheel her into the garden,
pigeons and sparrows peck anxiously
at the puddle of spilled grain.

This is where I find my way
along the well-worn path by the juniper,
sun diffused in diamonds through her straw hat.

It's as though we are viewing mountains
from a parked car, passing a thermos of tea,
pointing out the scrimshaw of eagles, as we really

study the rise and fall of spiders on silver threads,
thinking their travels too prone to random hits
but intrigued nonetheless by such industry.

I guess this is how it happens,
everything shrinking down,
the body, history, even scenery polished to their nubs.

She smiles as I hand her a bouquet of cosmos,
ignoring the white froth of bloom, she pulls from each
the tiny shining black seeds and places them in her pocket.

Childhood Inventions

We are back at the cabin
because this place has no wind,
no stony lakeshore or collapsed deck
where mallards come to raise a family.
So we are back at the cabin
where after dinner she places the thick needle
onto the black whirling grooves
and we dance on the pine floor,
spilt sugar and salt tossed over shoulders
swept beneath our shoes.
And I am wearing young-girl shoes
because this is not the place
that saw my later years,
the ones awkward with illness.
Because this is the place that molded
her mother's body, richly hipped
and moon-breasted in the sauna,
back to girl sidestroking the lake,
arms darting unthinkably fast
hollering at me to hurry up.
And because this is the place
where I would sleepwalk
and she would quietly follow me
out to the rowboat or the treehouse
or gently lift me off the bedpost
and walk me out under the stars,
rubbing out the clouds,
my small cold hands in hers.

Lily Fields

it was not the wind
you did not hear the bird
it was I
my thoughts
—Nils-Aslak Valkeapää

I try to read the dark alphabet of ink
along the white fields of your books,
but today they are only fields of cloud and ice.
You don't hear me as you lay awake on cotton sheets,
sweater woven in the downy under-white of owl wings,
your hair silver-cornsilk spilling over bleached pillows.
Eyes open, you focus past the newly washed walls,
pulled to the sunglow from the window
and you are not blindly looking,
you are seeing. And you begin to speak.
And as usual I am the one who is blind,
I do not see what you are pointing out,
because also I am unfortunately deaf
to the words you toss in such different jagged pieces,
but ones that come at me with such heat and color
that I can only think you have found that small rip
inside the curtain of your retina
that leads to some other landscape
that maybe holds hillsides in a momentary painting
where you reckless run inside the lilies.

The Stars Are Not in Her Counting

The stars are not in her counting,
to her they are but wandering holes...
—Ezra Pound

A wingbeat in the corner of the room,
I sit in attendance to your breaths
and to your mumblings that sound nothing
as much as the scuffing of shoes,
but with the volume turned up
giving voice to a language unknown to you,
like maybe Greek with its soft music that
floats like black martins into olive trees.
This is a foreign country.
The climate is mild, the language heavily inflected
but it is possible to do much with the gestures of hands and face.
The terrain is variable, which I am sometimes able to navigate,
but find I often lose my bearings. You are so small
and yet you have never seemed so large.
I find I wander through shops looking for trinkets:
bells, maps, candles, beads, jars,
something that gathers into offerings,
pictures of this life suspended between worlds,
something to help the selfish parts of me
that are easily lost and homesick.
Your calm face plowing silent Greek valleys
with the new shape of your words
mirrors another face I saw today tucked into a baby carrier.
Fuzzy-eyed and yawning, there you were
on the floor of the drugstore uttering the same bent vowels.
So the mortal coil flexes and reinvents.

Hands

The hand remembers:
I was a wing.
                              —Aleksander Wat

Often looking
for where they belong,
a purpose, the old life
filled with rapt attentions,

they are left
wringing disappointments
from sheets and blankets,
working hard at buttons and sleeves,

cradling each other like nesting cups,
reaching out to finger the invisible.
Birds of the stalled body,
they are given in confusion

and taken up by the sad, crude
snare of my own
where they spread their hollow bones
and retreat,

their rough wings
flying high
through thin clouds
always toward home.

Where There Is Singing

It all turns quiet here,
women fading to closure,
the angel-beauty growing
tired. It has come to this,
to these women, a cloudbank of widows
murmuring to themselves of old storms.
This is your family now
with whom you take your communion,
sing hymns of the body spent.

I place the books you have written into
your hands. You hold them with a sweet
separateness with which one would hold the idea
of winter never having known snow.

I ask you to sing
and you and I sing together,
the words ascend scales, climb high
where a swirl of notes gets deposited
and left abruptly. Two languages
settle in the air like steam
nurtured from stone.

I read you your words,
sing the other language.
You fix your gaze to place and time,
pull back, pull in,
fumbling in the dark.
What you want to forget
finally comes to you,
absence crowded with imperfection,
that old tongue.

Today while they are bathing you
I sit as you did, read the old runes.
The old poem brings me
to your childhood's silent days,
the immigrant suffering, thinning your bones.

Matalana maammostani
jäin kuin kiuruksi kivelle,
rastahaksi rauniolle,
kiuruna kivertämähän,
on mua kuuset kuulemassa,
hongan oksat oppimassa,
koivun lehvät lempimässä,
pihlajat pitelemässä.

Today you shook loose a long, low song,
with bended notes,
a floating picture I climbed into
as I would a boat pushed from a dock
like the many boats we kids rocked in,
canoes we carried, pulled on sand,
paddled eagerly away,
you on shore smiling, waving,
growing smaller,
among trees and sky,
you, just a fleck of white,
then gone.

Translation of the Finnish, from the Kalevala:

I have been without a mother
Like a lark on stone abandoned
Like a small thrush on a cairn
Left to sing there as a lark bird.
Only fir trees listen to me
Only pine boughs left to teach me
Tenderness I get from birch leaves
And caresses from the rowan.

White Rose

October was the time we pulled
the cover over the garden bed,
tucking in tight

shoulder to shoulder,
columbine and lemon balm
safe from the scarred hands of winter.

Beneath spill of saved eggshell, peelings,
clods of compost, the green bundles
waited patiently for their return.

I pile leaves into unruly mounds,
cursing the coming season,
hating the way silence fishtails in the cold.

Sitting by the broken willow
I think of how we used to eat apples on days like this,
throwing sculpted cores, betting on their future as trees.

I pick the last white rose of the season
from the spindly bush, its starry head
arguing light among the thorns.

Voyage, Orphan Dream

Swans circle and drop into cool sea water,
guide our boat to the distant island
where we step out into starflowers,
follow the worn path of sea oats
to the beach of blue stones.
You slice sour black bread, cover
small rice pies with clouds of egg butter.
We hold hands, rock to and fro,
you whisper chants by the fire,

Vilu mulle virttä virkkoi
sae saateli runoja.
Virttä toista tuulet toivat
meren aaltoset ajoivat.
Linnut liiteli sanoja
puien latvat lausehia.

You make my bed under birch-leaf quilts
and I sleep until the dawn thrums in my ears,
the single morning star locked overhead.
I walk the shoreline looking for you,
all I find are feathers left on stones.
I oar out again gathering the old days
into my hands, the names of things
I hunger and sorrow over
and let them all go back into the sea
where their ink is tasted and washed clean.

Translation of the Finnish, from the Kalevala:

The frost sang poems
The rain recited rhymes
Other poems the wind delivered
On the seawaves songs came drifting
Magic charms the birds brought forth
And the treetops incantations

82

Leaving

After she dies
all I can think to do is pick leaves,
to press in books,
set in clay pots in her memory,
roll up tight and slice for dumplings,
to make the reading fragrant,
the prayer more reverent,
the taste of sun, green in my mouth.

I take the leaves of bird cherry
and place them in my pillows
that I may dream a heaven tree,
a lake filled with green islands,
a rye flower hill to climb
and a birch-bark basket
into which I can place my worries,
unthreading them from my belt like beads.

I ladle water over leaves and rock
and soap my skin with birch
in the hot dark room
where my grandparents
pulled babies from mothers
and cleansed the bodies of the dead,
in the puff of steam I taste tree and bone.

Wearing our loose skins of sorrow,
our hair blown by north winds,
we kneel by the fern bank,
pull large cakes of dirt from pots
and plant long tongues of lilies,
knowing that just like the dried wings of sky,
the dense ocean of snow, a hunger for morning,
the pop of new red buds—
they too will come.

Star Moving through Nine Heavens

Another Saturday

Sitting in the yard, ignoring the garden rake,
I drink my tea and lie to myself
that I have nothing else to do.

Clouds of grackles churn the sky
with noise and wings, their irate chatter wasted
on the neighbor's cat who yawns and licks his belly.

I have left our bed, your deep breathing
opening and lifting the sheet
of your midday sleep.

I look at the birch trees,
their pale silver bamboo
slender stalks of a white moon.

Soon I will clip the baby leaves
and scatter them on our bed
as we get drunk by our own heat

and later run underneath the milk branches
letting the cool night air
tongue breezes on our skin.

Today dust whirls in the mudbank left from
last year's floods, the old house needs paint
and the gates half hang on hinges.

Our days appear and are gone again the same way
parachutists fall away from a plane at breakneck speeds,
the details lost in all the white silk.

But we know that is not the only way it is.
It is sometimes like this——you dreaming in Chinese,
pushing your oar into the Yangtze as you nap inside,

snoring and sighing under the candy-striped quilt
and I sitting out here with trees,
drinking my tea, one cup, one cup at a time.

Dance Lesson

You walk me backwards,
step one two, three, and four.
You grip my hands hard as if preventing me
from falling over some great precipice.
We stop breathing as we collide into other bodies,
the rhythm we are trying to map and retrace again
tumbling and rolling away from our feet.
It is New Year's Eve and we are scuffing our shoes
across the linoleum floor of the Danish Hall.
We are learning how to tango.
The social worker from the Veteran's hospital
says it is simple, just walk, guide your partner,
let your pelvises meet.
Looking at this group, the meeting of pelvises
is not a customary public endeavor.
It is simple, he says again. Just walk. Now rock, now dip.
But it isn't simple. We know what simple is.
Simple is hanging up on those ardent telemarketers,
letting the dental technician scrape your gums.
You step on my feet. I step on yours.
We turn in opposite directions.
The band plays Finnish tangos,
songs about sea birds, lost chances, harbor roses,
all the while the dance floor is cluttered with
tripping feet, couples lunging and lurching
like scores of giant carp snagged on fishing line.
I hear something in the far-off distance,
most likely the whole nation of Argentina throwing back
its perfectly postured head and howling.
We try again. You unclamp my hands,
I follow your steps, we sweep past the potluck table
groaning with unearthly concoctions.
Something is happening, passing over the same footprints,

the pattern worn smooth, our feet no longer seem to be wading
stiffly through an Arkansas mud bath,
our bodies no longer orphans of dank basements
and work cubicles with static-ridden telephones.
We have crossed over to the other world.
This is a country village and it is the grape harvest,
this is the night of the northern lights
and the reindeer are racing down the city streets,
this is the festival of the pearl divers,
lanterns and fireworks bloom a thousand coins into the sky.
The music ends and we let go.
We are lined up around the room like the new apostles,
some of us shrug and get a cup of coffee,
some of us fill plates with hard tack and havarti,
some of us sing in silent praise of our bodies
that proved to be taut and light as tambourines.
We will not preach for we have not the language
but we will carry in the stony field of our body's memory
the way the room pulsed, lifting the clouds to reveal the moon
big as an African drum and shimmering like abalone,
this dance born in the slums of Buenos Aires
and outlawed by the Pope,
born again in a Danish Hall in south Minneapolis,
taken to our flesh and pronounced into the quiet
dark morning of a new year.

Trying to Get Pregnant

I think of the time
we flew the kite above the sand dunes,
feeding the string to the wind, its nylon chambers
shimmering on the air current
even as it wrinkled and dropped like an empty purse.
As we shook off the sand grit
and ran it again down the water's edge, it flickered
like some elusive source of energy we couldn't touch.

We ran, gently tugging its imperceptible cord,
lining up the planets with its pink tail.
It blurred as it ascended, shining fish across the retina,
and as it faded, the sudden impulse to give it a name
as it ripped a deeper hole into the sky.

We stood below, old believers holding up its sign,
our bodies braced against the prevailing winds,
maneuvering ourselves into new directions,
always there for more string, uplift,
always there through the improbable flight and sag.

In the Infertility Clinic,
Studying a Photograph of Redwoods

It is like standing
In a river valley of Chinese gates,
Tall and massive

But missing true doors.
Here the doors are high branches
And our child and I pass

Tiny ants
Between the totems
That breathe dark syllables,

Great shafts of light,
And we are caught
In a quivering.

The same flash and dart that
Light the lamps of ginseng,
That gives the scroll painter

A state of grace
As he finds the vanishing point,
Fixes sunlight with his horizon.

But here there are no traceries,
Just trees that build beyond
Prayer sung in temples.

This is where
It still rings out, the birds
Pulling notes from nests,

Their children passed
Into a new vertical state,
Rising from the earth.

Rising hundreds of years,
Past kiss of pollen and moss,
Past song, past death, past cloud.

Tundra Swans

They feed on the wild celery,
a symposium of white wings
folding and unfolding old stories
while the snow is still nothing but seeds
banked in skies weeks away.
What makes us stand here like children
listening to them as if they were telling us
some fable we desperately needed to hear?

Winking and disappearing inside the reeds,
they spin the fairy tale
of persecution and resurrection,
the slippered girl in the silver tutu
pointing out that thin blue line
where life can cross back over on itself
as each season high spirals into the next.

Like a cloudburst set low between the hills
their many sudden shades of pearl,
cotton bloom, lily bulb, and ice floe
beat feet upon the water and go up
as if that was what water was for,
to launch yourself element to element.
Hundreds of swans leaving the tundra behind
burying their heads inside their wings
to sleep the curled sleep of snakes and cats
and all those classical *o*'s of nature that dazzle us
like dogs sleepless under a full moon.
Here in the steady surf of wings
shimmering in their finer orbits,
their black beaks drink it in,
drink at the great dark bowl of earth,
the same earth that shrinks at our touch

and swells to hold seas for their feasting.
And you and I standing here
watching the surface of the lake,
stunned by bird and sky,
thirsty for them.

Star Moving Through Nine Heavens

as we wait for our child

You point and say means good luck,
through the kitchen window
a thread of wild ducks
both fish and dragon flying south,
their backwoods hymn
a song of grasses stuck in new ice
as they pass beneath the Great Bear,
a trail of bird, then smoke.

We wait like those shorebirds
await the warm waves,
food drumming the sand,
only these months are bigger than wave,
than forest, than silence.
Only the sky seems big enough.

I make you get out of bed
and drive far out past the city,
its glow a distant hedge of candles
from the cornfield
as we stand inside the darkness
waiting for the northern lights.
Only a faint wash of white appears
and the silver minnows of a shooting star.

My rubber boots leave a zigzag of time,
lonely trail in March snow
where I filled the birdfeeder.
I notice how toe prints stitch the snow bank,
bird ghosts beside the fallen seed.
I feel the growing weight of distance.

We wonder at the empty spring earth
and what it will bring to us this year
besides raspberry canes and thick nests of chives.
I make soup with winter melons,
you show me how to write the Chinese words
for sun, peach, gold.

Summer arrives, the mother ship
unloading July cargo of scooters,
ice cream trucks, water balloons
dropped from the neighbor's tree house.
We study this geography for what it might hold
of hers. Mulberry, egret, kingfisher, plum? And always
the white stone brilliance of what we'll never know.

South of polar star, east of autumn
somewhere our daughter is being carried
in from the fields perhaps, from the river town,
past bramble gate, market, cooking fire,
past where the boatmen lean with piles of fishhooks
and bitter herbs, past busy streets and glass buildings,
her raven hair small wings inside her blanket,
her heart making tracks across the world.

Bosque del Apache

What we find here today
are two parents and a little girl
kneeling in a bed of New Mexico rock
watching the sky fill and drain of birds.
The child is far from the monks
who sang their low chants to her
in between giant apples and incense
in a different sacred place that also vibrated
with a foreign sound of god.
We find snow geese and sandhill cranes,
sudden bursts of arctic lilies and jointed flutes
opening and closing, the sky flooded
with an orderly tempest.
What finds us is the shadow drone of birdtalk,
a low rolling like a grand piano pushed onto a stage.
It is an under music that pulls us past wing,
past the whir and bugle
to a drift of tones deep inside our veins
where dreams score the blood
and sometimes come to light,
just as deep inside the dusty rubble hill
streaks of blue-green stone affirm themselves,
hidden prayers in the belly of the earth,
and just as men in saffron robes will bless wind,
bless grass, bless little girls
queued up for migration.
The child squints up at the pulse
of a thousand white wings
from her own bed of stones
as if angels flooding the foothills
is an everyday act of life,
as it should be,
as it is in certain holy swamps across the planet,

and then her head is bent back to her solid task,
first filling her parents' open hands
with the finer bits of broken rock
and then filling her own pockets with so many
of the small, sure offerings.

Ancient Wonders, the Modern World

I. In the Beginning

Sun flings itself against the curtains,
faces pressed to pillows
we feel the fingers of morning
the way the baker fingers the dough:
first soft and nudging, ending with great slaps.
We reach from our sleep to take the day,
legs emerge from the whipped foam of sheets
and there we are—
like that pair walking together in Laetoli
3.6 million years before.
We walk together to the bathroom mirror,
survey the damage, brush our teeth.
Threading our knuckles, foot bones
arching on the floor boards,
we waltz between the stove and refrigerator,
we peel and juice the morning fruit.

II. Peopling the Earth

The sky holds the moon,
a large golden plum,
foxtrots and sonnets,
proposals and midnight dips
founded under its ripening glow.
And we take to colonizing our flesh,
litter the bed with visions
of our bodies' invention.
As you brush my hair with your arm;
Is this how they did it?

Did they come together back then?
Neanderthal and Homo sapiens,
grinding under this same moon,
this way, breathing hard,
like this, as one?

III. Early Settlements

We climb the ladder through the ceiling trap door,
above it a bare room with one window
and banks of pink fiberglass.
Our first house and a space is untouched,
it may be all that will be left when we go
like those farmers in Çatal Hüyük
who settled and then abandoned their site, leaving
behind bull's heads, bone forks and spatulas.
When we move, this place of needle clouds,
bats and birds may be the only hint
as to who lived here—
the curled-up twine
of whispered love and hesitancy
sewn up inside the sparrow's empty nest.

IV. First Farmers

I score the black earth,
lift it out like wet coffee grounds.
While you spear clods and level beds,
I cut holes in the dark crumble
and fill the deep mouths with corn flowers.
You press seeds—butter beans, lettuce,

pumpkin and red peppers.
We wait at its side
as if it were an ocean making a wave.
Complete with night crawlers,
crabgrass and potato bugs,
to us, this garden is flawless.
We are like the Minoan farmers,
we pour from a vessel the fruits of our harvest,
we eat them with a pleasure unhinged
to any known words,
we eat them with homage,
we eat well.

V. Origins of Writing

Fingers black and sticky,
I sit in this solitary narrow chair
spilling the salt and flowers
of ink figures onto paper.
You read these,
you keep them.
They are not the clay tablets of Elba,
they are not the gold votive tablets of Pyrgi,
they are not Chinese oracle bones.
They are
signal, listing, record, symbol,
picture, keyhole, journey, shadow,
mistake, gaze, honk, spinnings,
pylon, chalk lines, thicket, bubblings,
murmur, salvo, longing, promise.

VI. Acts of Faith

Here at this table filled with bowls
we come to answer our own prayers
in feast, in belief, in presence of our
own silence. Here where the universe
balloons outward from our tongues
and comes back down to the smallness
of fish bones and seeds on our plates.
You and I tell of the day's labor,
the ice-chilled roads,
work shot wild with old troubles.
And we accept the unburdening and relief
while dissolving the unwanted, keep as written
praise the world for its sun and birds.
We continue to find not just in dreamsleep
or in the nest in the berry bush
but in the eyes and lips and fingers of each other.
Here is sanctuary, here is refuge,
here where we are safe from the snow-fed winds,
where our bowls are full of the tender grain
and where later you and I like the blue herons
moving down from the clouds
will fall to bed and touch the ground, singing.

Acknowledgments

I would like to thank the Minnesota State Arts Board for the fellowship grant that allowed me all the opportunities and hours to work on this book. So much gratitude goes to all my writing friends who patiently read and helped edit the majority of the poems in this book. To all the wise women of Onionskins for their generosity, humor, and keen eyes. To the Bedford poets who showed me the best places to prune my wild things. To John Reinhard's poetry newsletter and those looming monthly deadlines that forced me to just shut up and write. Thank you also to John Krumberger who helped me to stay honest and tender with the section about my mother. And to Mary Kay Rummel who willingly read the entire manuscript and offered smart questions and kind advice. To Monica Ochtrup who has mysterious powers and vision when it comes to finding themes and order. Thanks to Börje Vähämäki for permission to reprint the epigraph "Go To the Forest," by Tommy Tabermann (English translation by Börje Vähämäki), published in *Treasury of Finnish Love: Poems, Quotations, & Proverbs: In Finnish, Swedish and English*, Börje Vähämäki, editor (Hippocrene Books, 1996). And to all the great staff at New Rivers Press, thank you for your many hours of skill, commitment, and dedication in making this lovely book.

The following poems, some in earlier versions, have appeared in these publications:

"Sketchbook of a Trapper's Wife" in Water~Stone

"In the Deep Woods," "Dance Lessons," "Tundra Swans," and "Where There is Singing" in *Collecting Souls—Finnish Voices in North America*

"Hunger" in *i.e. magazine* (selected by Edward Hirsch)

"Tuula's Nettle Soup" in *Sampo the Magic Mill*

"Digging Lupines" and "*Finlandia*" in *The New World Finn*

"Ancient Wonders, the Modern World" as *Ancient Wonders, the Modern World* (Red Dragonfly Press)

"Night Walk to the Sauna" in *To Sing Along the Way: Minnesota Women Poets from Pre-Territorial Days to the Present*

Biography

Diane Jarvenpa is a Minnesota native whose grandparents all emigrated from Finland. Her first book, *Divining the Landscape*, was published by New Rivers Press in 1996. She has received grants from the Minnesota State Arts Board and, as Diane Jarvi, is a versatile performer of folk and world music heard throughout Europe, Australia, and the United States.

Praise for The Tender Wild Things

"From the first lines of *The Tender Wild Things*, you'll know you're in the hands
of a master chanteuse and poet. Among the most magnificent of these poems
about family and place are those written to the mother, whose bonds to the
poet are made of light and song, tradition and language. That the women share
a Finnish heritage, that their paths often led through woods, gives the poems
flavor and a particularity; that they sing from the heart makes the poems into the
'small planets' we all live on. Reading . . . *Wild Things* is experiencing that sweet
delight in finding another book to fall in love with."

—Sharon Chmielarz, author of *The Rhubarb King*

"An uncanny northern magic flows from the pages of *The Tender Wild
Things*, at once earthy, celestial, and deeply mythic. Diane Jarvenpa's book
is, to quote one of her poems, 'a giant humidor of words and images.'
Ah, but what words, what images! These wonderful poems, musical to their core,
drive unerringly toward the higher intensities of incantation and spell."

—Thomas R. Smith, author of *Waking Before Dawn*